Big Sailor

My First Big ABC

Ages 3-5

Vol.5 M·N·O

Acornidu!
Your study buddy

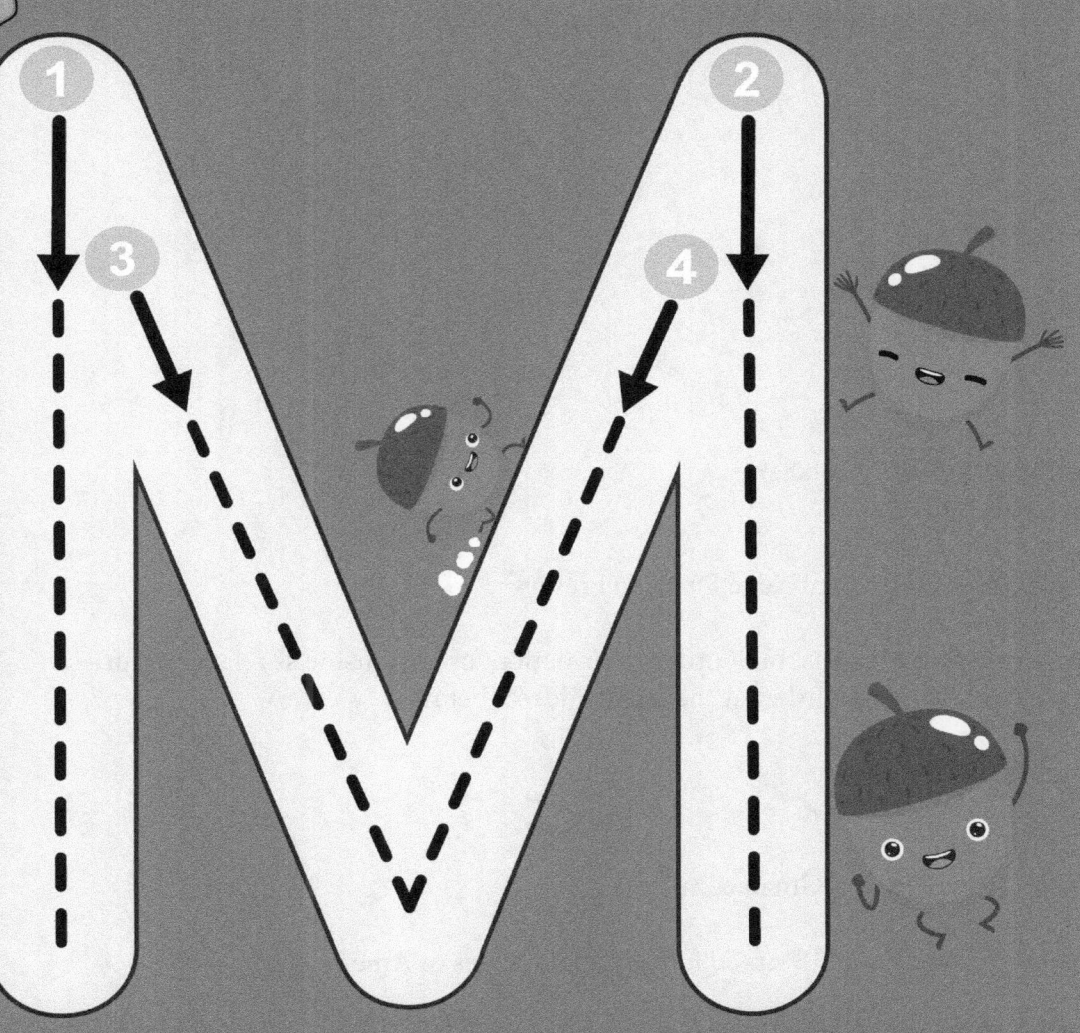

My First Big ABC Book Series
Big Sailor Edu

Copyright © 2021 Cambridge Dynasty Press

For permission requests, bulk order information, or any busine ss related inquries, please contact the publisher at the email address below.

Cambridge Dynasty Press
30 N Gould St. STE4000
Sheridan, WY 82801
Email: Bestsailoredu@Gmail.com

Written, Designed, and Printed in the United States of America

978-1-7357844-7-2(Paperback)

47678459

Hi! Nice to meet you.
My name is Acornidu!

I am your study buddy for this book!

1. Building Skills for Pen Control
2. Recognizing Alphabet Letters
3. Building Confidence
4. Enjoying a Good Book
5. Being Patient with Practice
6. Developing Creative Thinking
7. Being Proud of Achievement
8. Having Fun

This book belongs to

_____
(name)

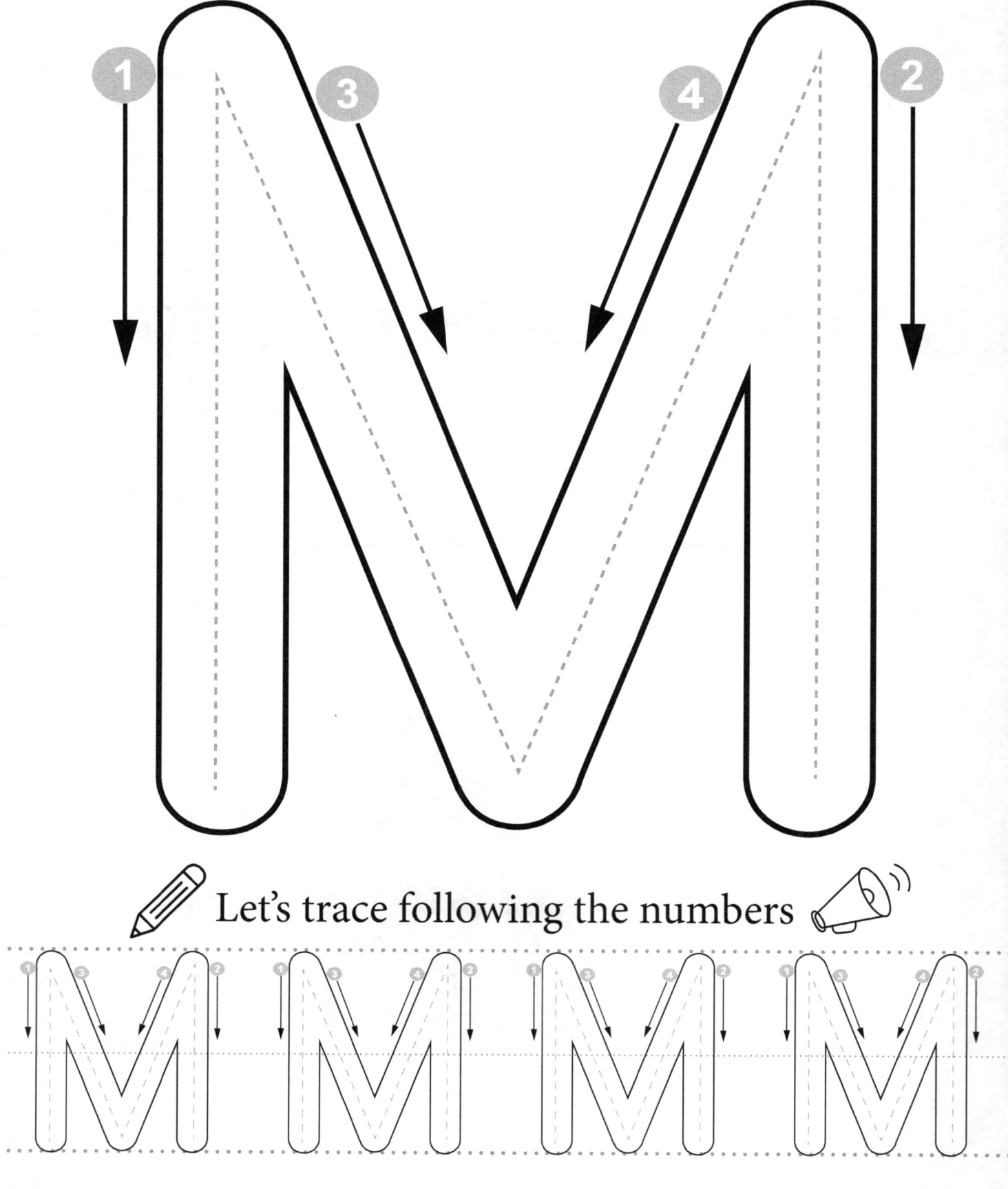

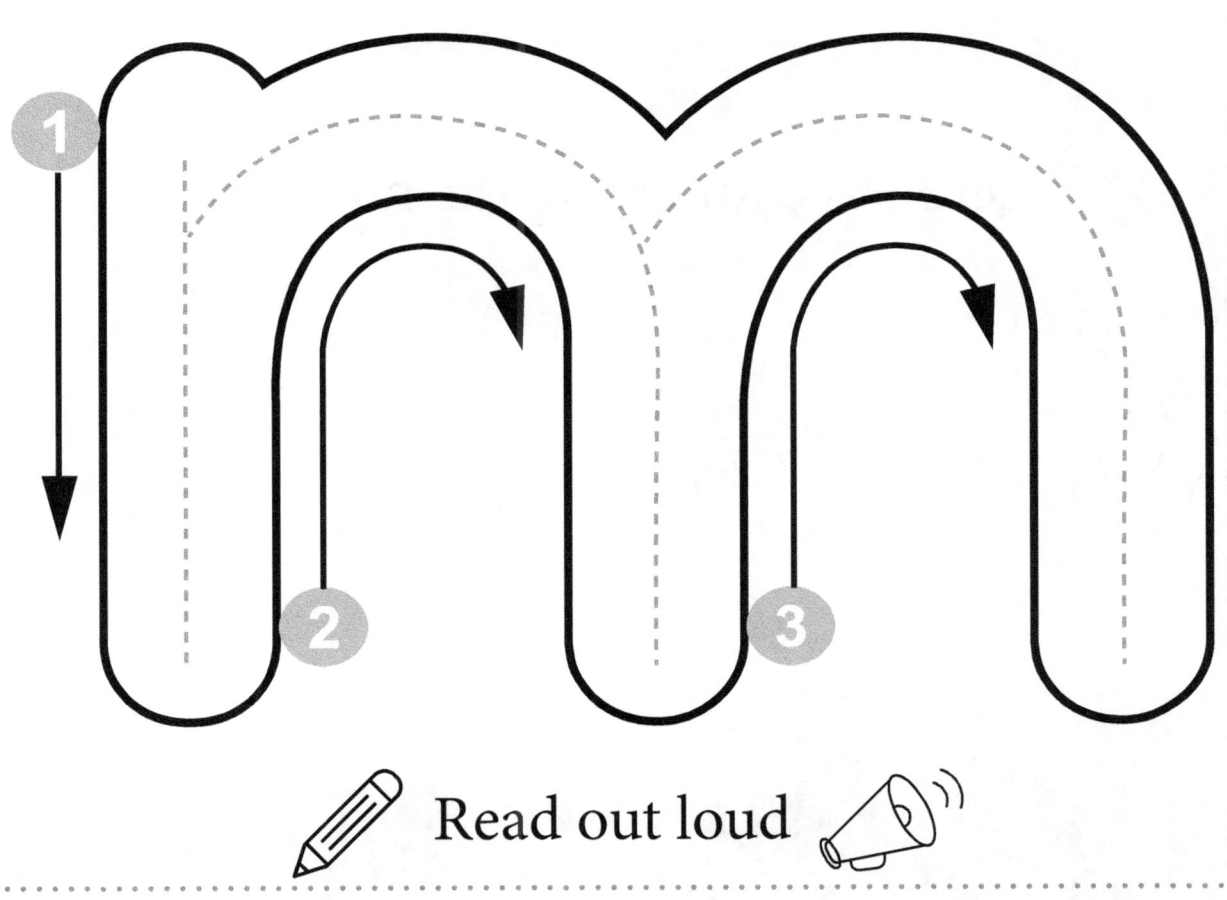

✏️ Read out loud 📢

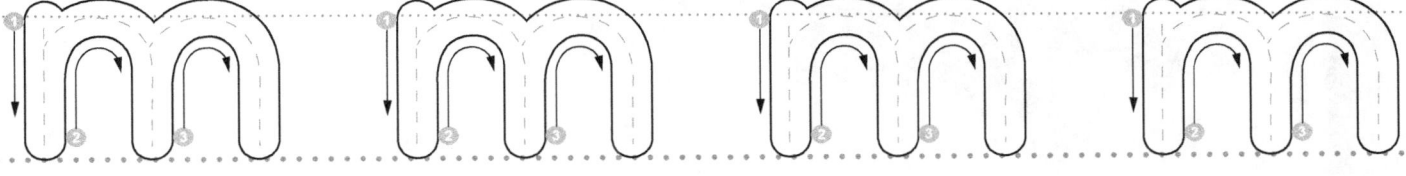

Milk

✏️ Let's trace following the numbers

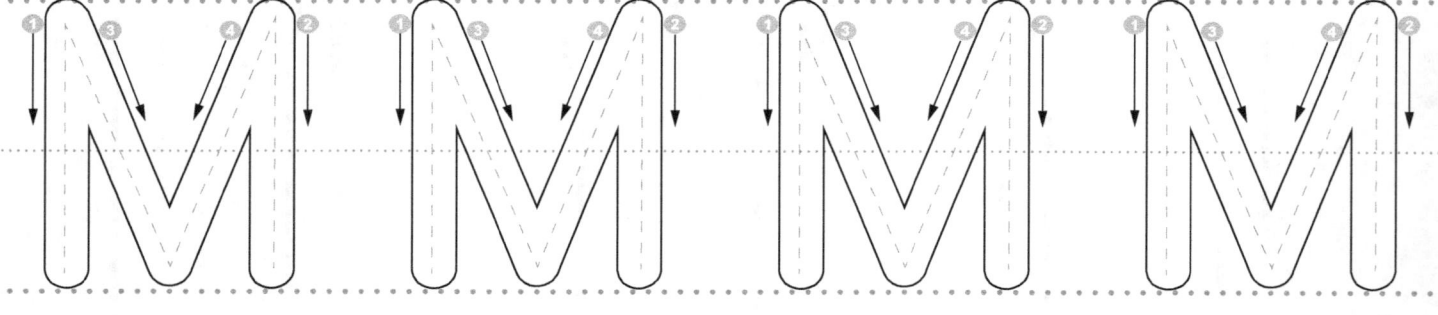

Mouse

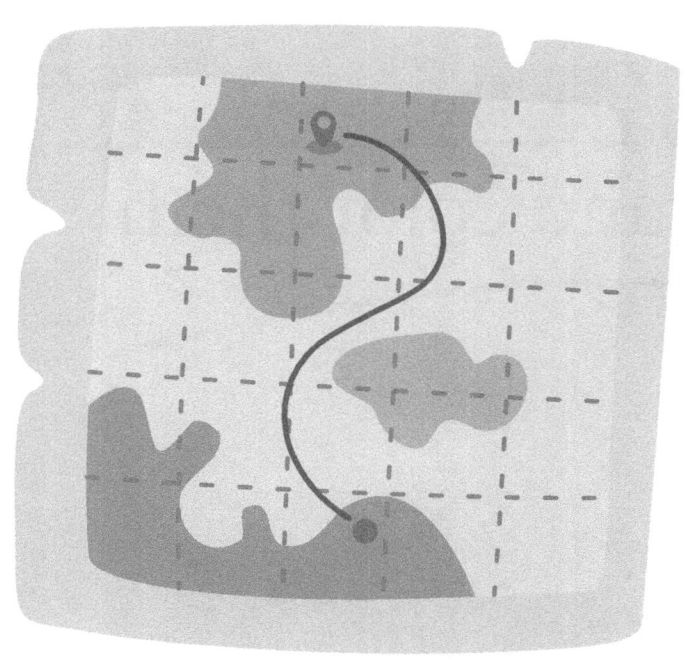

map

 Read out loud

m m m m m

mushroom

Find every M and color them

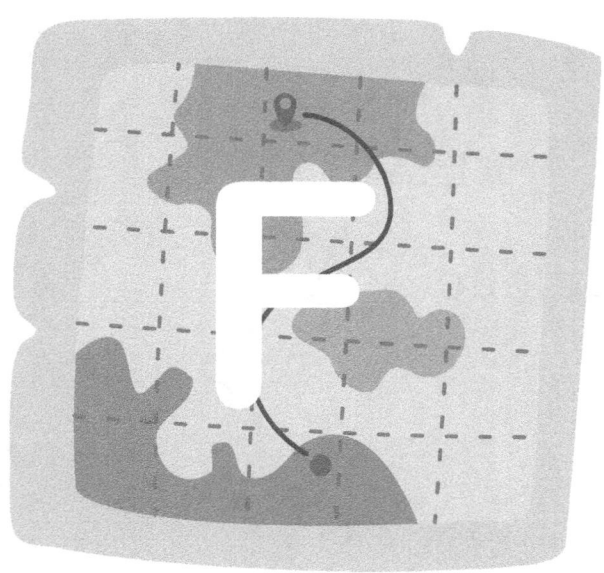
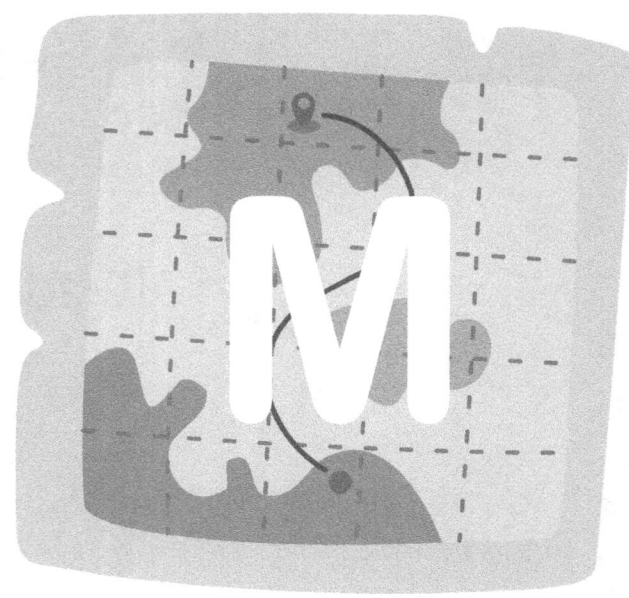
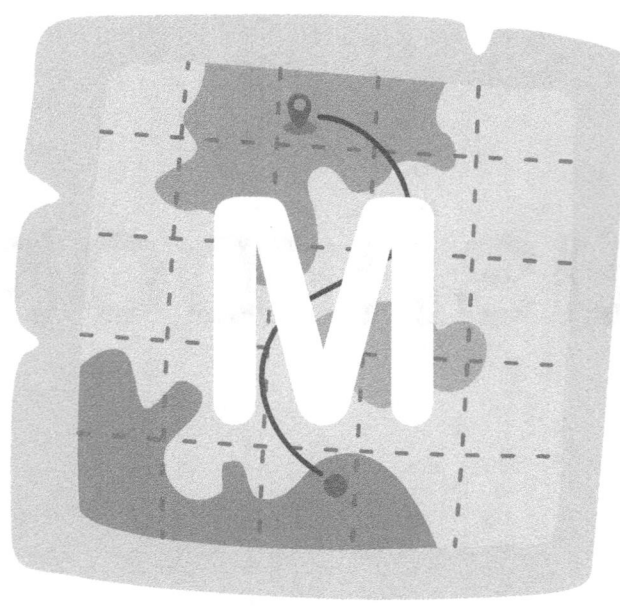
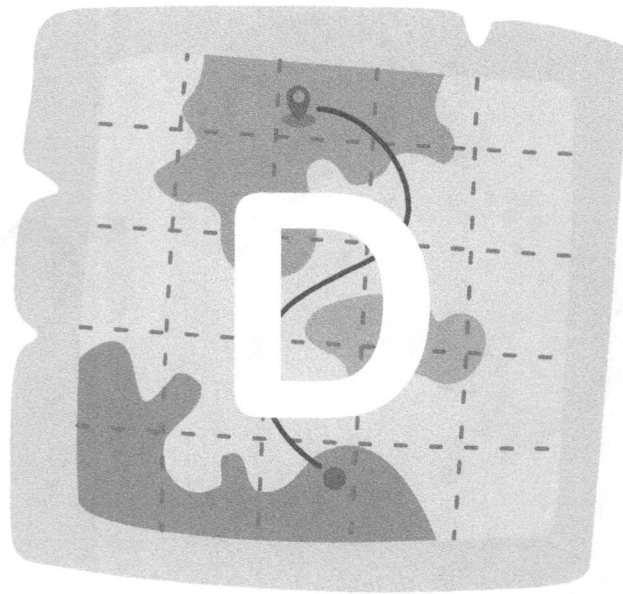

Trace the dotted line and read out loud

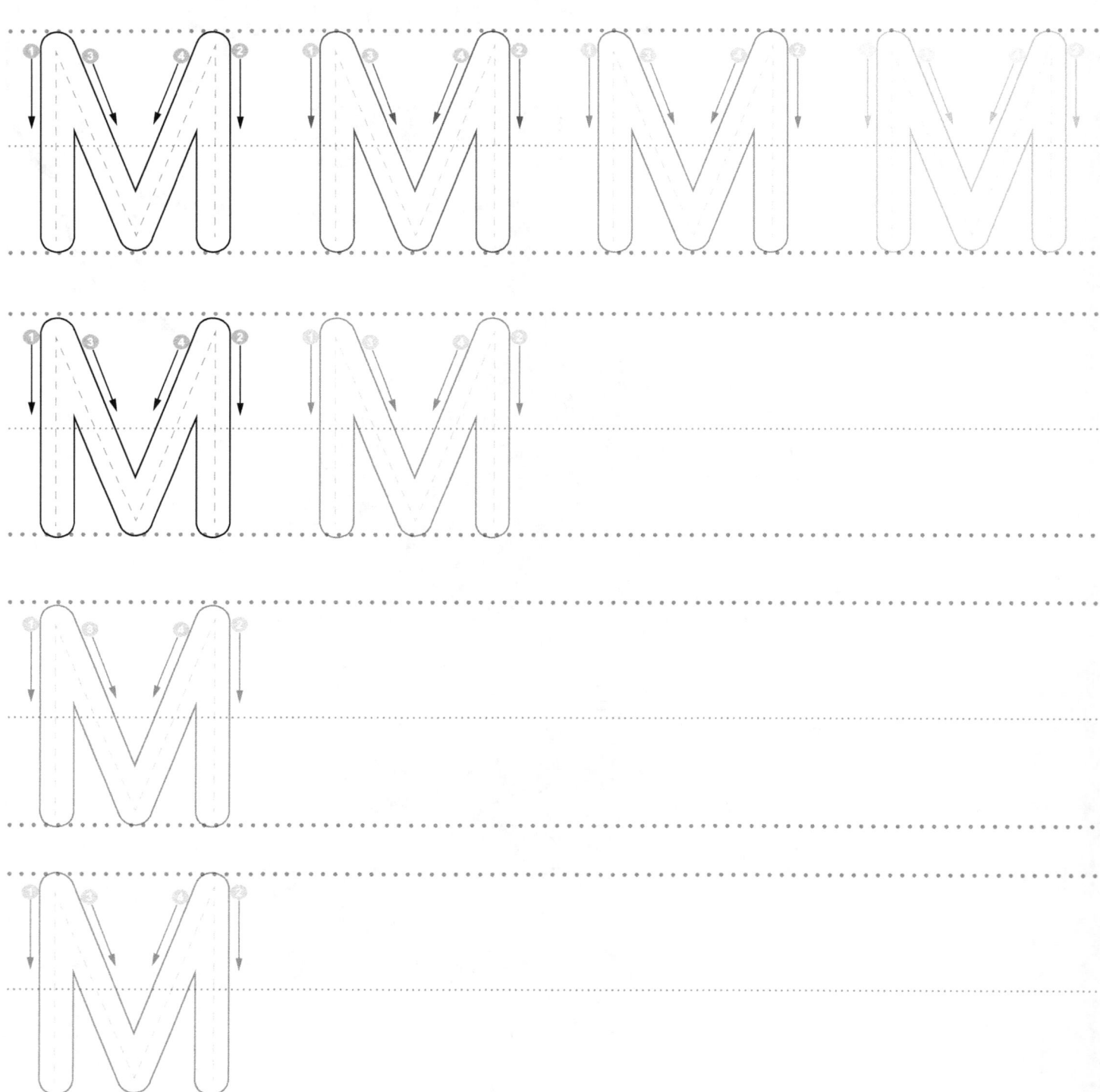

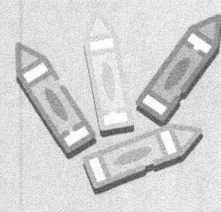 Find every M and color the sections

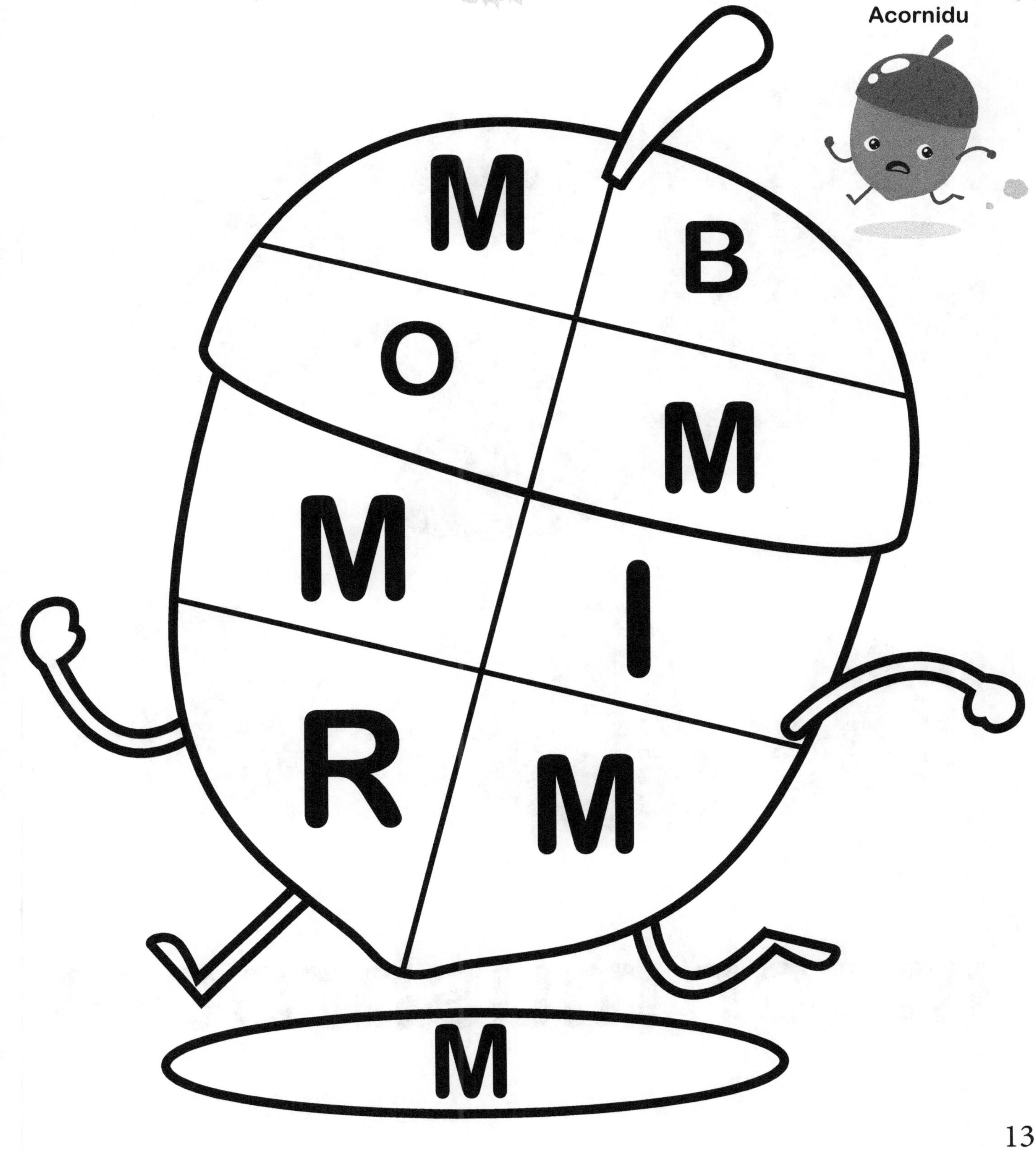

Find every m and circle them

m for mushroom

Trace the dotted line and read out loud

M for Mouse

Draw lines to match

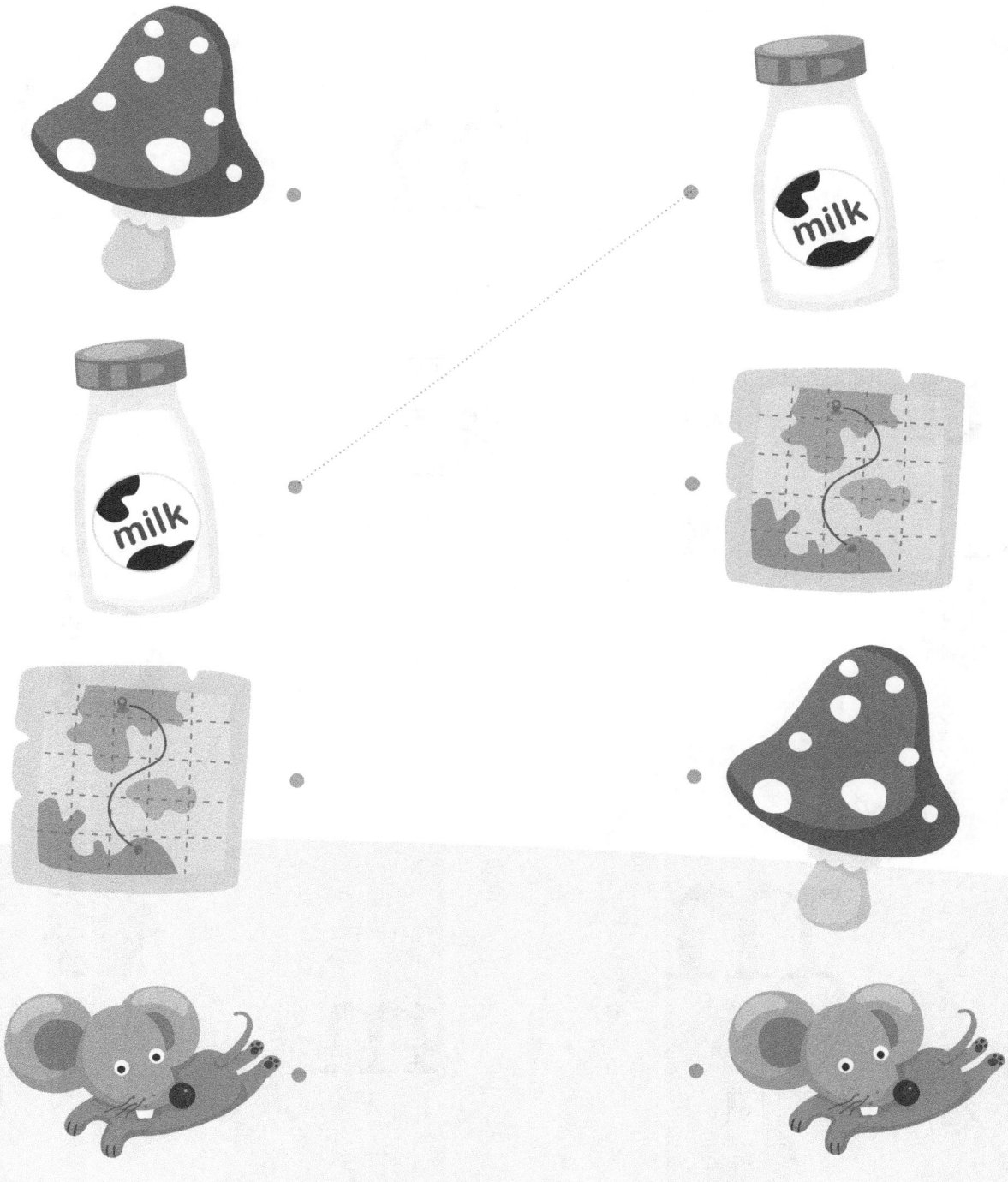

17

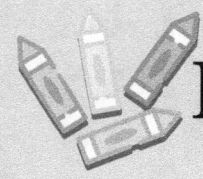 Find every m and color the sections

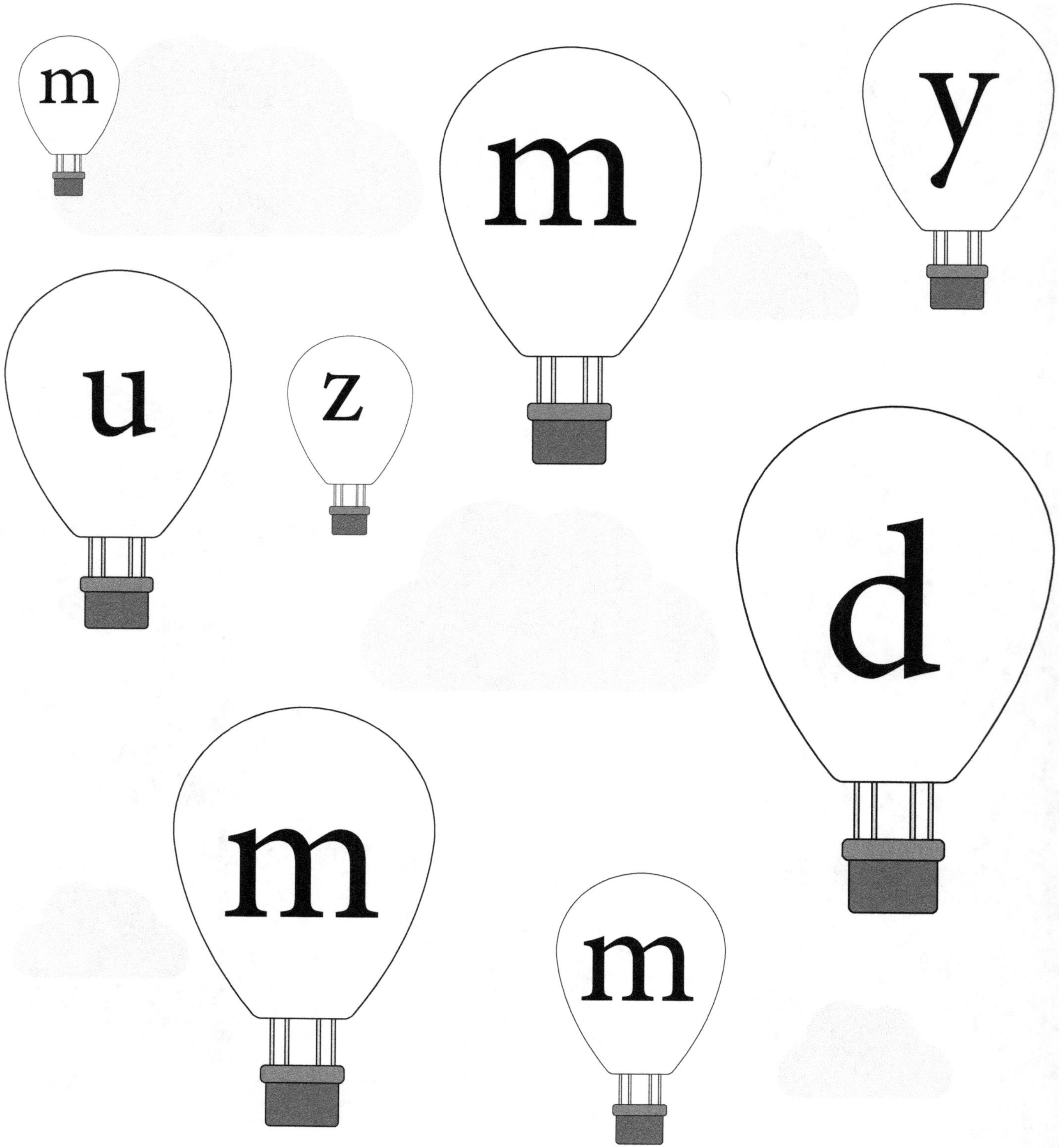

Trace the dotted line and read out loud

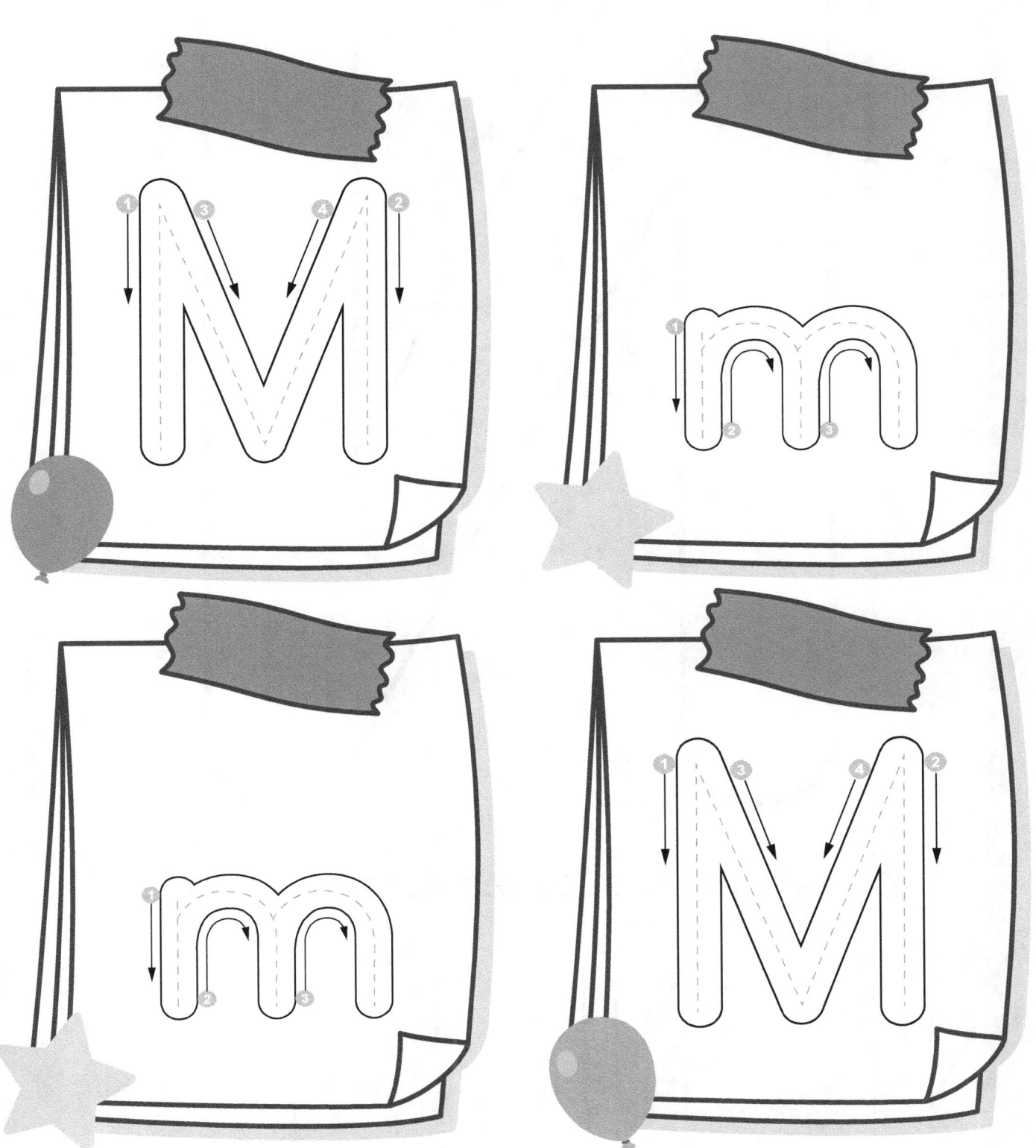

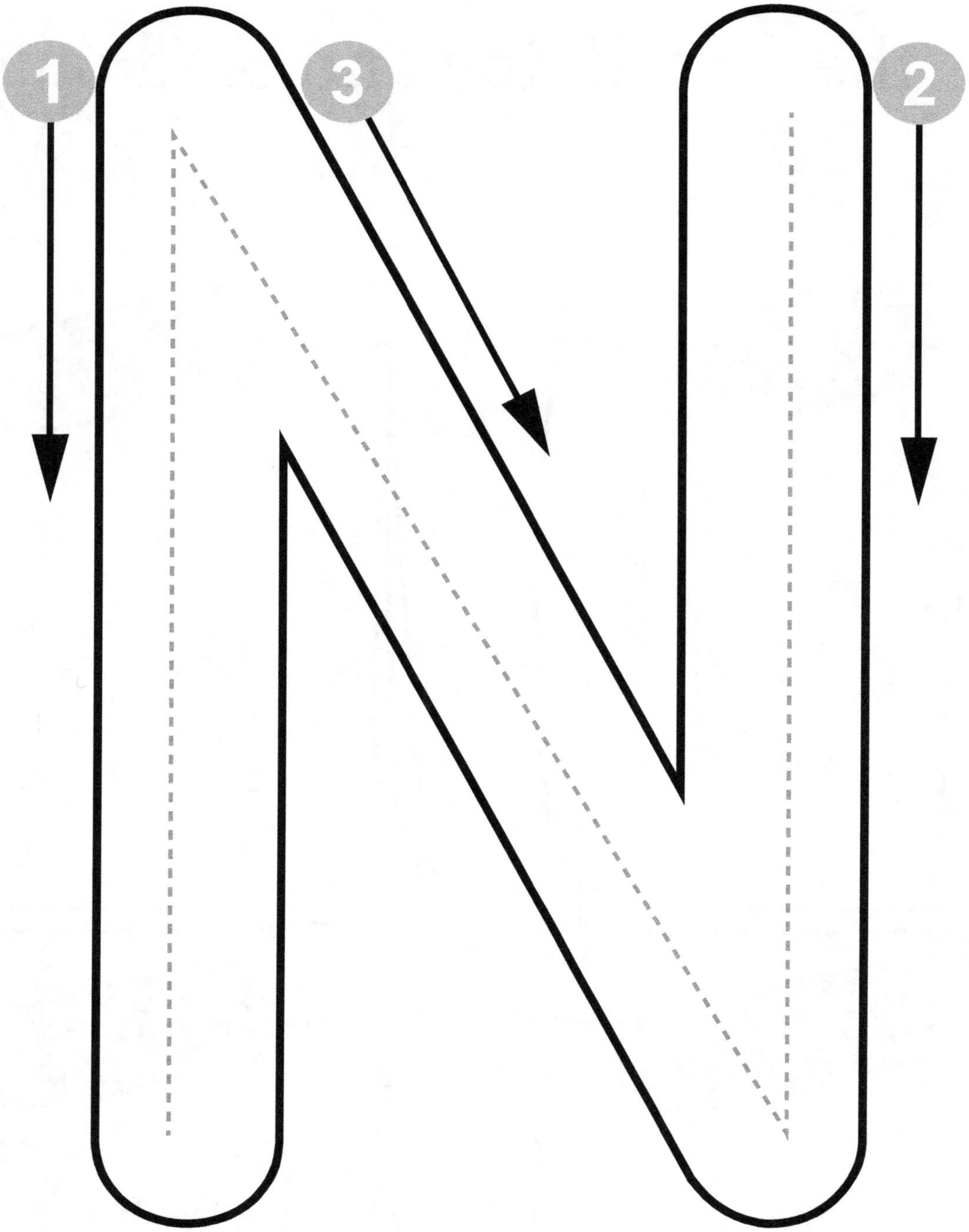

Let's trace following the numbers

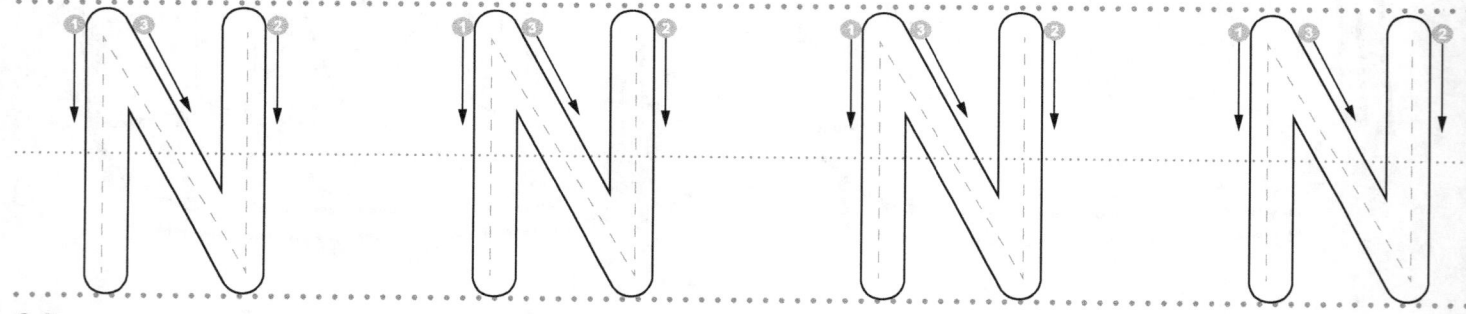

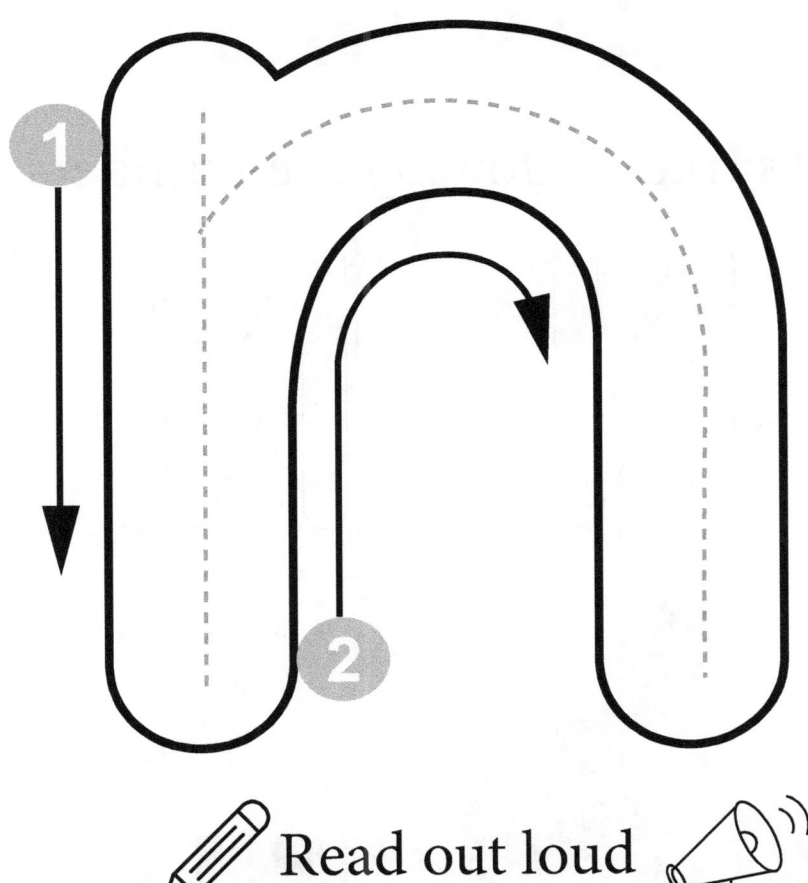

 Read out loud

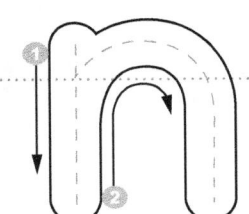 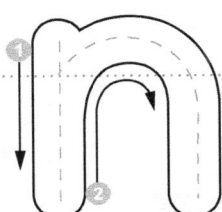 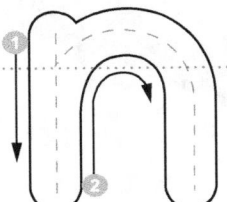 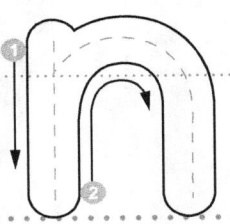

Narwhal

 Let's trace following the numbers

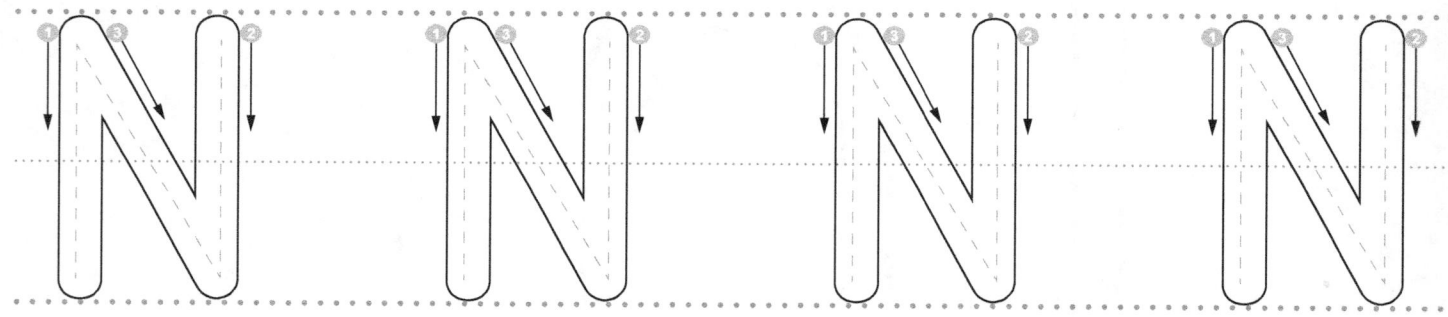

Nest

net

 Read out loud

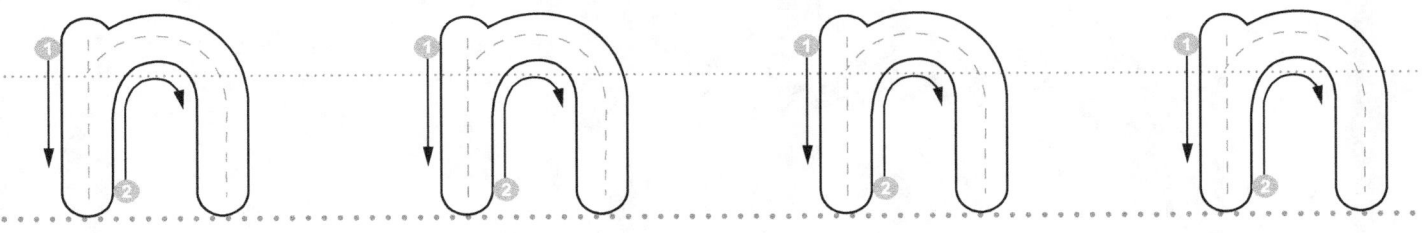

nut

23

Find every N and color them

Trace the dotted line and read out loud

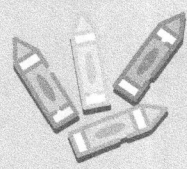 # Find every N and color the sections

Find every n and circle them

n for nut

Trace the dotted line and read out loud

Draw lines to match

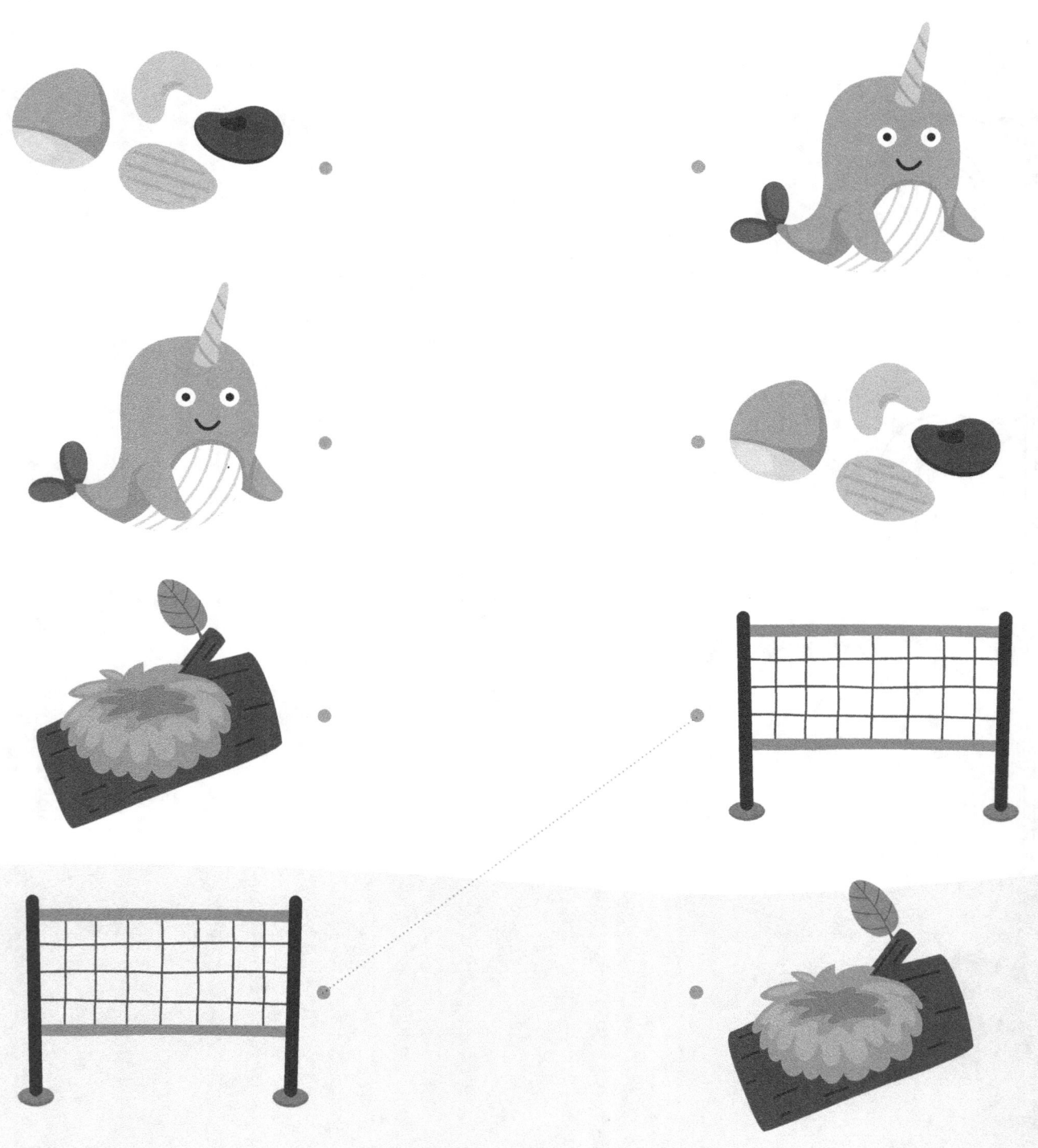

N for Narwhal

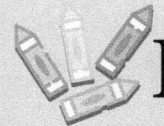 # Find every N and color the sections

Trace the dotted line and read out loud

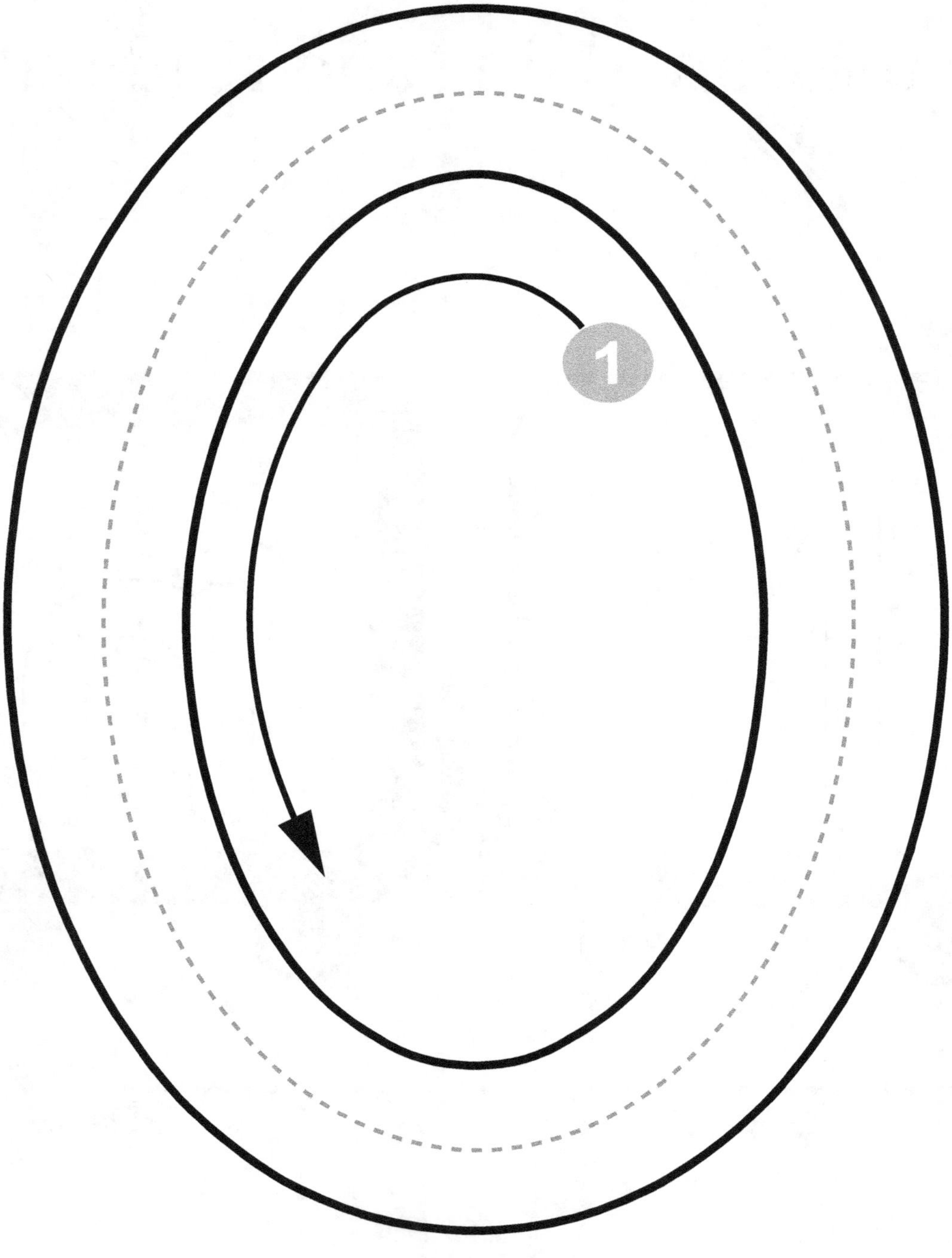

 Let's trace following the numbers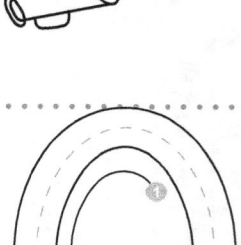

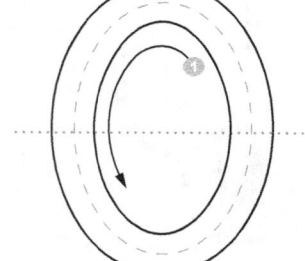 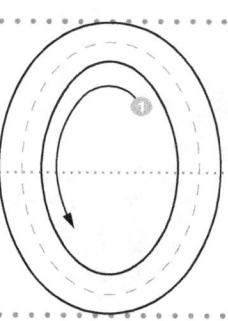 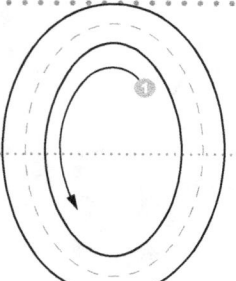 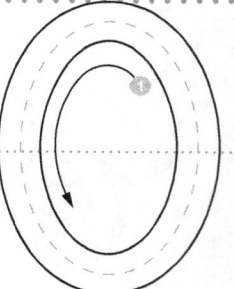

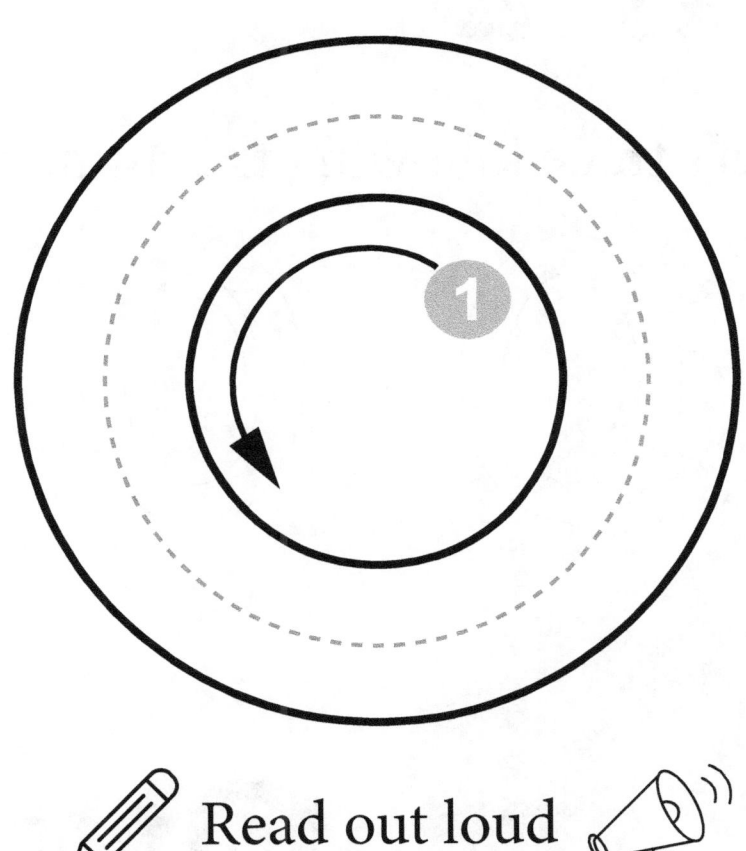

 Read out loud

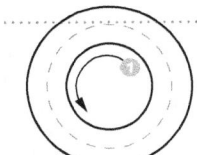 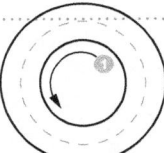 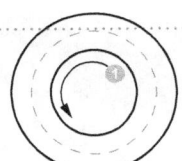 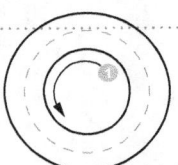

Owl

 Let's trace following the numbers

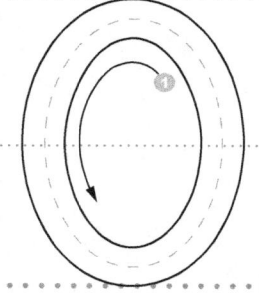 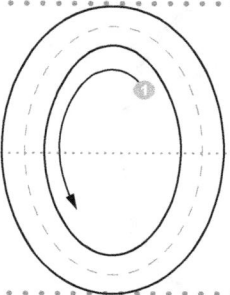 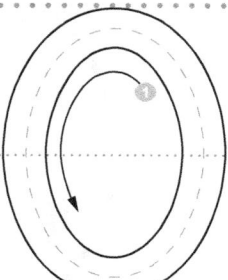 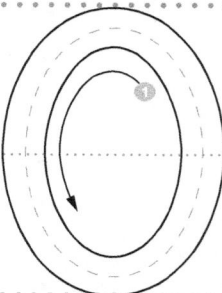

Oyster

✏️ Read out loud 📢

○ ○ ○ ○

Find every O and color them

Trace the dotted line and read out loud

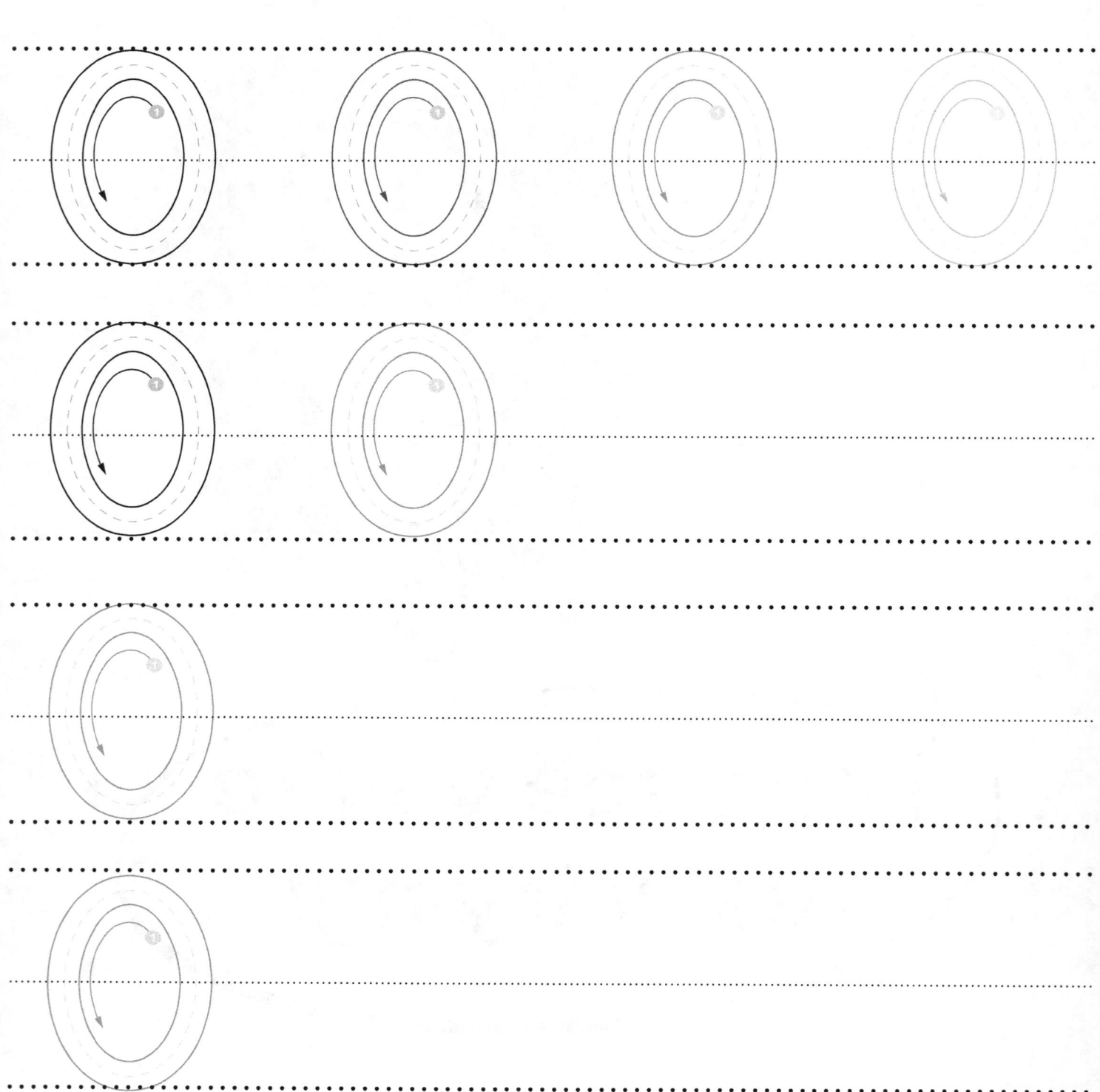

Find every O and color the sections

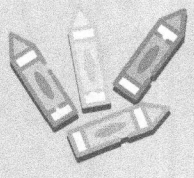

Acornidu

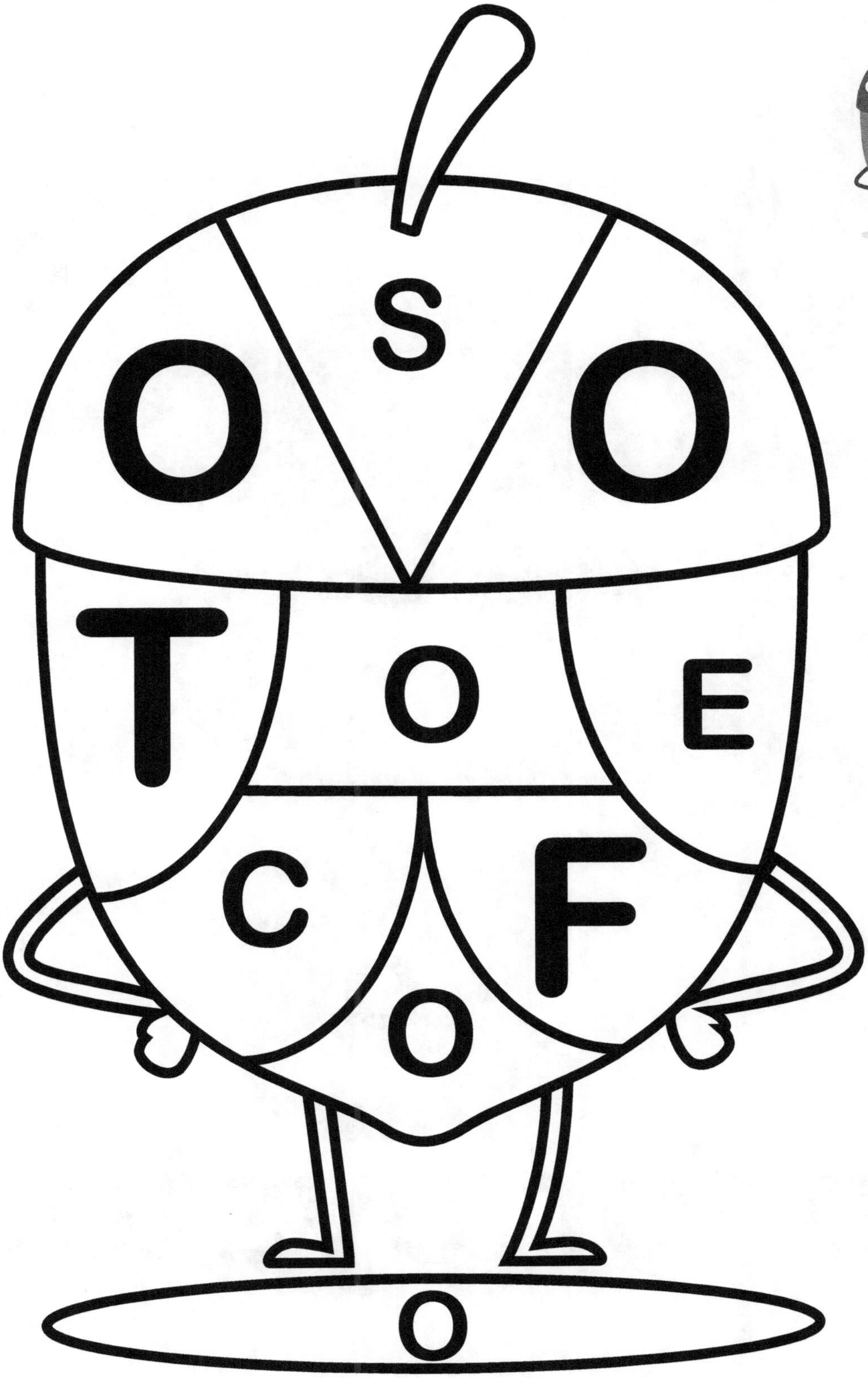

Find every o and circle them

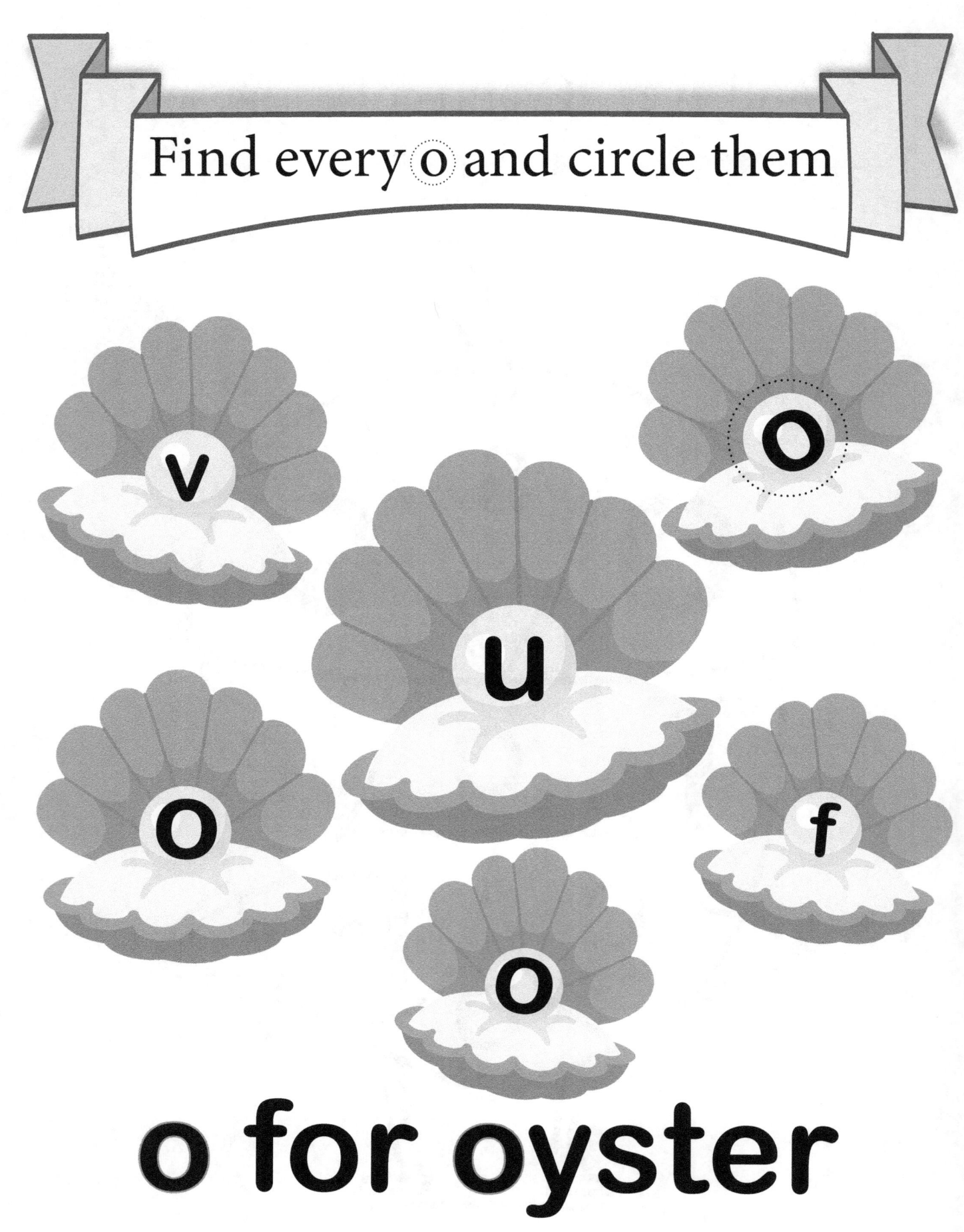

o for oyster

Trace the dotted line and read out loud

O for Owl

Draw lines to match

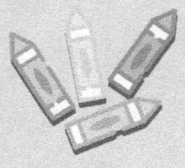 **Find every o and color the sections**

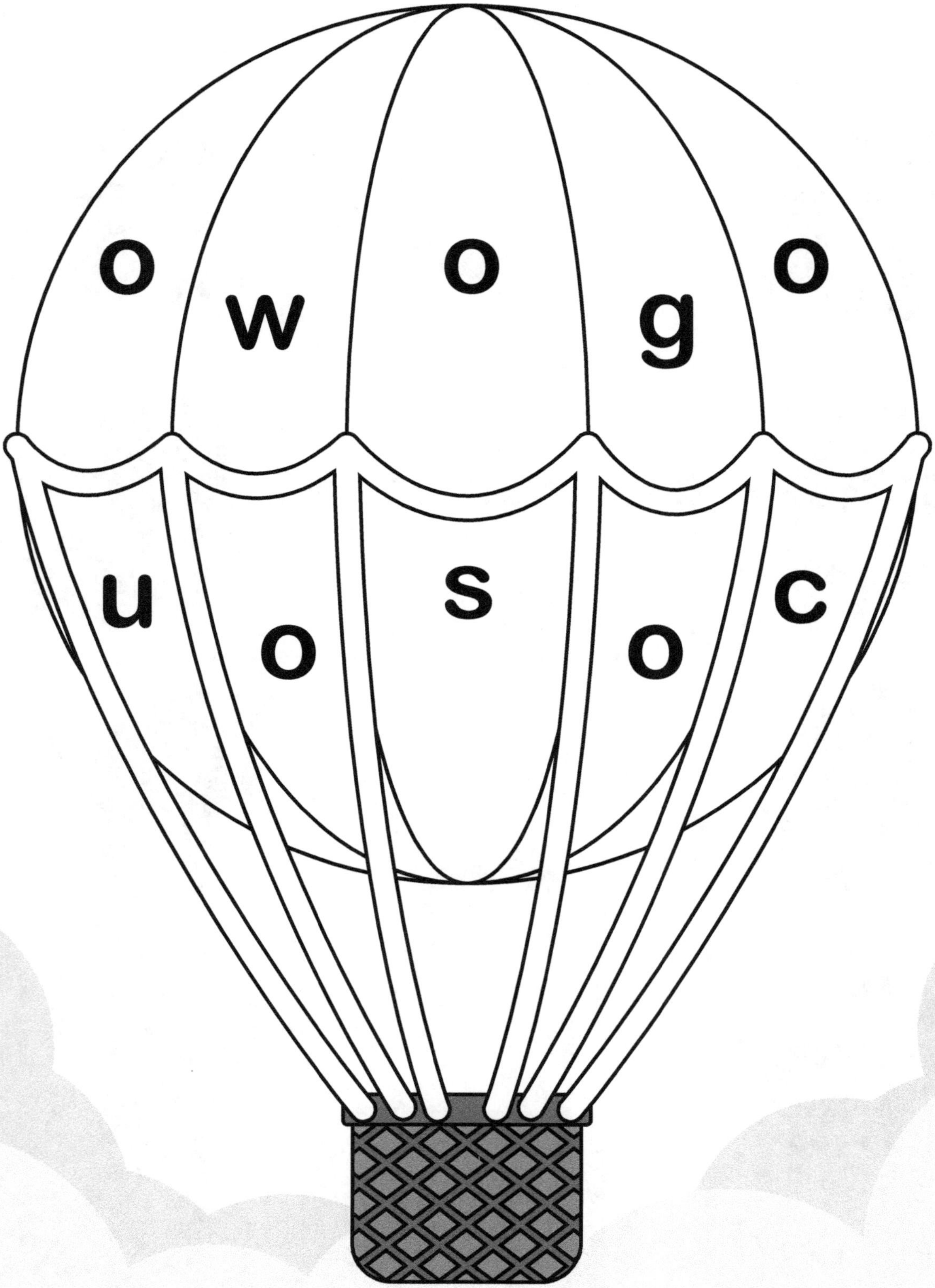

Trace the dotted line and read out loud

Where is Acornidu?

Find and circle!

Let's express your

I am cool

I am hungry

I am playful

I am proud

I am okay

feelings with Acornidu!

I am tired

I am excited

I am loved

I am confident

I am happy

Let's express your

I am sad

I am calm

I am rushing

I am frustrated

I am angry

feelings with Acornidu!

I am strong

I am embarrased

I am confused

I am shy

I am brave

Write MNO and read out loud

MNOMNO

MNO

MNO

MNO

Write mno and read out loud

Award

You are amazing!

This award is for

_____ _____
(first name) (last name)

Great job finishing the book!

Date: _____

Visit Our Website

BigSailorEdu.com

and Get Free & Fun

Educational Material

ABC Workbook Series by Big Sailor Edu

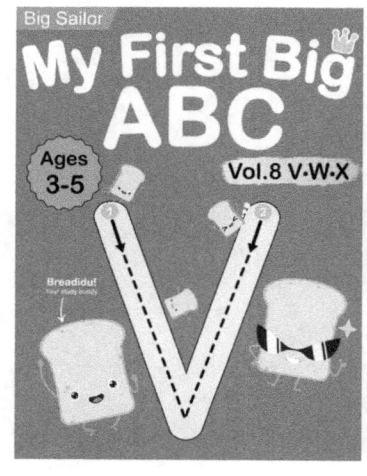

Cambridge Dynasty Press

www.ingramcontent.com/pod-product-compliance
Lightning Source LLC
Chambersburg PA
CBHW081422080526
44589CB00016B/2629